WANDERING WILLOW
IN SPAIN

By Brigette Burgman

*Dedicated
to the explorers, wanderers,
and curious-hearted; and to all the
incredible people, places, and cultures
that make this world so beautiful.
Never stop Wandering.*

Hola, bonjour, hello, my little one!
Let's go on an adventure, let's go have some fun!
My name is Wandering Willow,
I like to boogie across the world,
learn about the cultures of all the boys and girls.
I like to swim in oceans, oh-so-crystal blue,
dance through sandy deserts, and howl at the Moon!

I have a wish to travel far,
but how I travel is not by car!
I'd like to take you on an adventure with me.
I promise you'll love all the things we'll see!
Hop on my earth-ship made of treasures from my travels,
and see all the beauty this world has to unravel!
Do you want to know something, my friend?
My favorite part of an adventure is actually the end!
I know that sounds strange, but it's true, come with me
now and I'll show you...

ZOOOOOOOOM SPAIN!!

Arriving on a Spanish beach, who do I meet?
I'm greeted by a crab crawling up my feet!
"Hola, bonita, me llamo Marcos the Crab.
Would you like me to show you
all around this enchanted land?"
We dance along the Mediterranean Sea with glee.
"This will be so fun!" I say. "Hurray! Yippie!"

We go to a bakery, it smells so sweet,
Marcos shows me pastries, which the locals eat.
"They are eaten for desayuno every day,
filled with chocolate, the yummiest filling, they say!"

We dance down streets, surrounded by so much art.
Seeing the artist Gaudi's work is my favorite part!
We reach a place with a church rising high in the air.
"How long do you think it's been being built there?"
Marcos asks. "Guess, if you dare!"

133 years!
With 10 more to go.
No wonder people pass
by saying, "Wooah!"
Standing so tall, like a
castle of a king,
La Sagrada Familia,
what a magical thing.

Marcos then takes me to a big stadium ring.
"Bull fighting in Spain is a well-known thing.

It's a tradition, which has been going on for years,
it can be dangerous for the bulls and sometimes end in tears!"

It's time for flamenco — a traditional dance,
it's harder than it looks at first glance.
It's fast, a guitar strums and people clap,
women wear beautiful dresses that flap.

Marcos turns to me and asks me for this dance,
so we have a happy crab prance!
People welcome us with kisses on each cheek.
It's the traditional Spanish meet and greet!

Marcos says, "Let's go for almuerzo, which is lunch.
People here take their time to enjoy their crunch!
Dining can last for hours on end,
as Spanish people enjoy a meal with friends."

He orders us a dish
called paella!
"What in the world is
paella I say-aaaa?"
Marcos replies,
"A mix of shrimp, fish,
and meat, rice and
veggies. Come on,
let's eat!"

"Willow, my little wandering dear,
we're starting to run out of time, I fear.
What else haven't I taught you about this magical land?"

Marcos asks then takes me by the hand.
"This is futbol, it's how they say soccer in Spain.
The Spanish love to watch and play the game."
Marcos finds a ball, and kicks it my way.

Marcos shouts, "It's time for dinner!
This one will sure be a winner!"
We have tapas — lots of little plates of food to share,
and eat until we're stuffed and the plates are bare!
When I see churros con chocolate, I give a big grin,
I'm sure my tummy can fit them in!

My belly is full, and so is my heart.
Now comes the goodbye, not an easy part.
Marcos and I dance back down to the beach.
I'll remember all he's said and all he did teach.
We say our farewells, I place him back in the sea,
and think of all the things he's shown me.

Remember right back at the start,
I said the end is actually my favorite part?
This adventure has shown me new things,
and with that lots of memories it brings.
When I'm at home, lying in bed,
I can travel in the memories within my head.

Adios amigo means goodbye friend!
But always remember goodbyes are never the end.
The friends we meet will stay in our hearts,
we won't ever truly be apart.
Join me again for an adventure in a magical land.
Will it be in a busy city or a desert with sand?
You'll find out next time, that's for sure,
because there's just so much to explore!

Always remember, my little shining star,
that you are special and can travel far.
Go see the forests, the desert, gaze up at the stars,
reach for the Moon, reach for Mars!
Filling your days with beauty as you travel,
will open up the world and adventure will unravel.

WOOSH!

A gust of wind washes over me.
I watch my hat leave my head and flee.
"Hat, hat, please come back to me!
We have more adventures to have together, more to see!"
I hope it shows up while wandering my next magical land.
Where I go next is unknown,
life never seems to stay as planned.
I plead with the sky to bring my hat back to me.
Where I'll find it next, we will have to wait and see...

COMPREHENSION QUESTIONS

1. How do you say lunch in Spanish?

2. What is the name of the famous church they visit?

3. What is a traditional dance called in Spain?

4. What is a common dish in Spain that they eat for dinner?

5. How do you say friend in Spanish?

AUTHOR BIO

Brigette Burgman is a professional photographer, storyteller, and travel enthusiast who spends half her time in Chicago and the other half traveling to various places around the world. Brigette runs a photography company, Nomadic Soul Photography, specializing in destination weddings and elopements, and capturing various landscapes, which she turns into fine art. The tales of Wandering Willow are inspired by Brigette's real-life travels to different countries. She aims to write one for every country she has visited, to help teach children about different cultures around the world and inspire them to travel themselves!

Printed in the United States of America
First Printing: May, 2022
ISBN: 979-8-89109-227-3 - paperback
ISBN: 979-8-89109-228-0 - ebook
ISBN: 979-8-89109-520-5 hardcover